FREUDIAN SLIPS

S. Harris

RUTGERS UNIVERSITY PRESS
New Brunswick, New Jersey, and London

FREUDIAN SLIPS

Cartoons on Psychology
Sidney Harris

Library of Congress Cataloging-in-Publication Data

Harris, Sidney.
    Freudian slips : cartoons on psychology / Sidney Harris.
      p.   cm.
    ISBN 0-8135-2478-4 (alk. paper)
     1. Psychology—Caricatures and cartoons. 2. Ameri-
can wit and humor, Pictorial. I. Title.
    NC1429.H33315A4 1997
    741.5'973—dc21
                                    97-27345
                                        CIP

British Cataloging-in-Publication information available

Most of the cartoons in this book have been previously
published and copyrighted by the following publications:
*American Scientist, The Chronicle of Higher Education,
Fantasy and Science Fiction, Harvard Business Review,
Hippocrates, Medical Economics, Medical Tribune, The
New Yorker, Playboy, Practical Psychology, Psychiatric
News, Punch, Science, Science 85,* and *The Wall Street
Journal.*

Manufactured in the United States of America

FREUDIAN
SLIPS

"GREG FEELS HE NOW HAS THE ANSWER. ALL PEOPLE, HE BELIEVES, ARE PARODYING THEMSELVES."

"DELUSIONS OF GRANDEUR?
I AM GRAND!"

"SURE I'M DEPRESSED. I HAVEN'T HIT A GRAND-SLAM HOME RUN IN TWENTY-SEVEN YEARS."

"WHAT REALLY ANNOYS ME IS THAT THEY'RE NOT EVEN MY DEMONS—THEY'RE GOYA'S AND HIERONYMUS BOSCH'S AND BREUGHEL'S."

"SEE — IT'S NOT IMPOSSIBLE
FOR AN OBSESSIVE-COMPULSIVE TO GET A RESPONSIBLE JOB."

"IF WE DIDN'T DO SO WELL IN THE EASY BOX, THEY WOULDN'T HAVE GIVEN US THIS COMPLICATED BOX."

"MR. KILGORE, I HAVE REASON TO BELIEVE YOUR LACTOSE INTOLERANCE IS PSYCHOLOGICAL."

"WE COULDN'T GET A PSYCHIATRIST, BUT PERHAPS YOU'D LIKE TO TALK ABOUT YOUR SKIN. DR. PERRY HERE IS A DERMATOLOGIST."

"I CAN'T REMEMBER THE LAST TIME I TREATED A CASE OF AMNESIA, AND I CAN'T EVEN REMEMBER IF I EVER *DID* TREAT ONE."

"MY ASTROLOGER SAYS ONE THING, MY GURU SAYS ANOTHER, MY PSYCHIATRIST SAYS SOMETHING ELSE — I DON'T KNOW <u>WHO</u> TO TURN TO ANYMORE."

"WHAT DO YOU MEAN, WE SHOULD JOIN THE MEN'S MOVEMENT AND HAVE A MEETING? THIS IS A MEETING OF THE MEN'S MOVEMENT!"

"VERY WELL, I'LL INTRODUCE YOU. EGO, MEET ID. NOW GET BACK TO WORK."

"ACCORDING TO THE VOICE-STRESS ANALYZER, HE'S _NOT_ GOING TO LOWER TAXES."

"MELVIN, THIS IS DR. ROGATZ. I ASKED HIM TO DROP IN AND HAVE A LOOK AT YOUR DOODLES."

"HE SALIVATES."

"LET'S START BY DETERMINING THE TYPE OF PERSON YOU ARE. ARE YOU UPFRONT, OR DO YOU GIVE OFF SUBTLE SIGNALS?"

"I'M AT MY WIT'S END. YESTERDAY WALLY DECIDED TO BECOME A TRANSVESTITE."

"REMEMBER, MAN DOES NOT LIVE BY SPIRITUAL ENLIGHTENMENT ALONE. I'VE ALREADY MADE MY BUNDLE."

"DON'T YOU REALIZE, JASON, THAT WHEN YOU THROW FURNITURE OUT THE WINDOW AND TIE YOUR SISTER TO A TREE, YOU MAKE MOMMY AND DADDY VERY SAD?"

"THERE ARE ESSENTIALLY FOUR BASIC FORMS FOR A JOKE— THE CONCEALING OF KNOWLEDGE LATER REVEALED, THE SUBSTITUTION OF ONE CONCEPT FOR ANOTHER, AN UNEXPECTED CONCLUSION TO A LOGICAL PROGRESSION, AND SLIPPING ON A BANANA PEEL."

ATTEMPTING TO UNDERSTAND THE MARKET: MERRILL, LYNCH, PIERCE, FENNER & FREUD

"TYPICAL 'TYPE A' BEHAVIOR."

"YOUR CASE IS EXTREMELY INTERESTING, AND I WOULD LIKE YOUR PERMISSION TO WRITE IT UP AS A SCREENPLAY, AND ATTEMPT TO GET IT PRODUCED. OF COURSE YOUR TRUE IDENTITY WILL NOT BE REVEALED. IT WOULD UNDOUBTEDLY HAVE A WIDE APPEAL TO THE GENERAL PUBLIC AND THE SPECIALIST. IT WILL BE A COMEDY."

"A LOVELY DAY, A GOOD MEAL, AND, THANK HEAVEN, NO GUILT."

"BUT YOU MUST ADMIT HALLUCINATIONS ARE MORE <u>INTERESTING</u> THAN DEPRESSION."

"I CAUSE ANXIETY? BUT I HAVE ANXIETY."

"MR. HASTINGS CAN'T COME TO THE PHONE RIGHT NOW. HE'S MEDITATING."

"DON'T YOU SEE RICK — YOUR SLUMP IS JUST A SUCCESS NEUROSIS. YOU FOUND YOUR .394 AVERAGE DANGEROUS, BECAUSE YOU FANTASIED THAT IT WOULD BRING ABOUT RESENTMENT."

"HAVE A COUPLE OF DREAMS, AND CALL ME IN THE MORNING."

WHEN HE HEARD HE LOST ALL HIS MONEY IN THE MARKET, HIS HAIR TURNED GRAY OVERNIGHT...

THE NEXT DAY HE DISCOVERED THERE WAS A COMPUTER ERROR, AND HE WAS NOT WIPED OUT, BUT HIS HAIR DID NOT TURN DARK AGAIN

"OH, YEAH! MY SELF-HELP GROUP KNOWS A LOT MORE THAN YOUR PSYCHIATRIST. FIRST OF ALL, THERE'S A LOT MORE OF THEM."

"NO, THE BOOK YOU WANT ISN'T IN OUR SELF-HELP SECTION. IT'S PROBABLY UNDER PERSONAL GROWTH OR FINDING YOURSELF OR POSSIBLY EGO AWARENESS."

NEVER FORGETS

SOMETIMES FORGETS

ALWAYS FORGETS

"ALL I WANT FROM THEM IS A SIMPLE MAJORITY ON THINGS."

Q. HOW MANY PESSIMISTS DOES IT TAKE TO LIGHT ONE LITTLE CANDLE?

A. PESSIMISTS CANNOT DO IT. ONLY OPTIMISTS CAN LIGHT ONE LITTLE CANDLE.

"I'M NOT JUST A SOCIAL WORKER, I'M A PSYCHIATRIC SOCIAL WORKER. PERHAPS WE COULD DISCUSS YOUR EARLY CHILDHOOD."

"THAT'S WHAT COMES FROM HANGING AROUND
ALL THOSE APES — YOU'RE SUFFERING FROM A
SPECIES-IDENTITY CONFLICT."

"ON THE CONTRARY, I CAN'T RECALL A THING FROM FIFTY YEARS AGO, BUT I REMEMBER EXACTLY WHAT I HAD FOR LUNCH YESTERDAY."

...then the tree walked away, and I said good-bye to it... what a dumb dream... whose idea was it to analyze myself?... ach, it was my idea.
S. Harris

"FRANKLY, I'M DUBIOUS ABOUT AMALGAMATED SMELTING AND REFINING PLEADING INNOCENT TO THEIR ANTI-TRUST VIOLATION DUE TO INSANITY."

"NOW I'VE TOLD YOU TIME AND AGAIN THAT YOUR SYMPTOMS ARE IMAGINARY."

"YOU'RE NOT GOING TO GET YOUR WAY, NORTON, AND I DON'T CARE IF YOU ARE AN ONLY CHILD."

"I'LL TELL YOU IF YOU TELL ME — WHEN NO ONE ELSE IS HOME, DO YOU TALK TO HIM A LOT?"

"MY INNER CHILD JUST TURNED SIXTY-FIVE."

My lawyer says it's OK to jaywalk.
My mother says I can make faces if I want to
My minister says I can do whatever I want.
My doctor says I can be rude if I feel like it.
S. Harris

"ANALYZE YOUR HOSTILITY. EXAMINE YOUR AGGRESSION. WEIGH YOUR ANGER. IF THAT DOESN'T HELP, THEN THREATEN TO LICK ANY MAN IN THE HOUSE."

"REMEMBER — EVEN WHEN YOU LOSE YOUR PERSONAL SPACE, YOU STILL HAVE YOUR PSYCHIC SPACE."

IF YOU WERE AN ICEBERG...
THE PART EVERYONE GETS TO SEE
ALL THE GREAT ASPECTS OF YOUR PERSONALITY
S. Harris

"I DON'T WANT TO SAY HELLO TO ANYONE OR THANK ANYONE. THAT'S THE KIND OF GUY I AM, AND THAT'S WHY I WIN FIGHTS."

"WHEN YOU SIT DOWN, YOU GET A SHOCK. OPEN A BOOK, YOU GET A SHOCK. WRITE SOMETHING, ANOTHER SHOCK. IT'S A TYPICAL PSYCHOLOGY CLASS."

"ROGER DOESN'T USE THE LEFT SIDE OF HIS BRAIN OR THE RIGHT SIDE. HE JUST USES THE MIDDLE."

"IS IT FOR COERCION, EXPLOITATION OR PATRONAGE — OR IS IT JUST FOR SOMEONE YOU LIKE?"

"ON SOME OF THE PAINTINGS MY RIGHT BRAIN SAYS THEY'RE GOOD ART, BUT MY LEFT BRAIN SAYS THEY'RE BAD INVESTMENTS. ON OTHERS, MY RIGHT BRAIN SAYS THEY'RE BAD ART, BUT MY LEFT BRAIN SAYS THEY'RE GOOD INVESTMENTS."

"CAUSED, NO DOUBT, BY SOME FEELING OF MASS GUILT."

"I CAN UNDERSTAND MY MOTHER AND MY FIRST-GRADE TEACHER BEING THERE, BUT THERE'S ALSO A TV ANNOUNCER WHO DOES DOG FOOD COMMERCIALS, AND A SECOND-STRING CATCHER FOR THE DETROIT TIGERS."

"I'LL HAVE TO GET DR. KENDRICK TO REDUCE HIS DOSAGE OF PROZAC."

"I WAS BEGINNING TO THINK OF MYSELF AS A VISIONARY. TURNED OUT THEY WERE HALLUCINATIONS."

"DO PEOPLE HATE US BECAUSE WE DRESS THIS WAY, OR DO WE DRESS THIS WAY BECAUSE PEOPLE HATE US?"

"SURPRISINGLY ENOUGH, THE ACT OF UPHOLSTERING A SOFA IS SYMBOLIC FOR THE ACT OF UPHOLSTERING A SOFA."

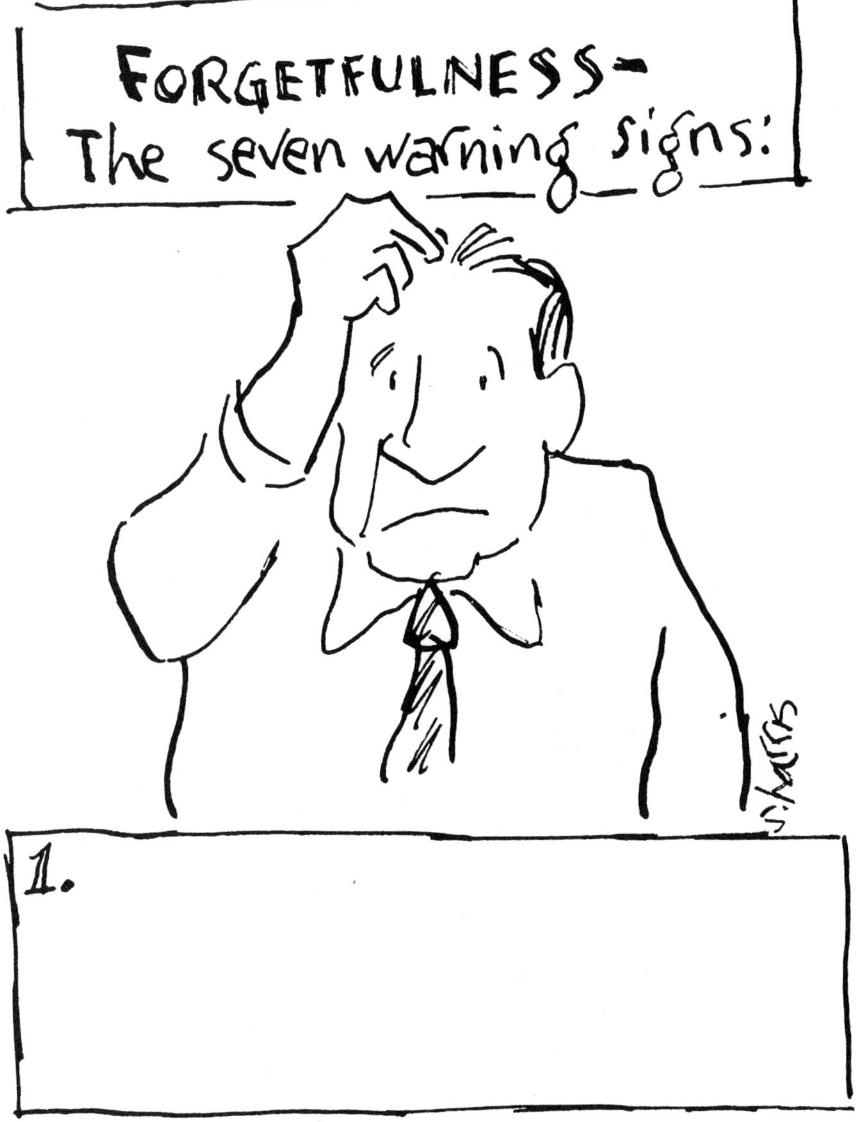
FORGETFULNESS-
The seven warning signs:
1.

"LISTEN– IT'S PSYCHOANALYSIS COMING UP THE RIVER FROM VIENNA."

"...AND I'D LIKE YOU TO MEET MY WIFE, MY EGO, MY CONSCIENCE, MY AMBITION..."

AN UNEXAMINED LIFE

AN EXAMINED LIFE

"WITH A ONE-MAN BUSINESS, IT'S MURDER BEING A MANIC-DEPRESSIVE."

"DR. GOTTSCHALK, I JUST HAD THIS REMARKABLE DREAM, AND I WAS WONDERING IF YOU COULD COME RIGHT OVER AND ANALYZE IT."

"IT'S A NEW SYSTEM. I STEP ON SOME CRACKS, AND I DON'T STEP ON OTHERS."

"THIS IS NOT ABOUT ORIGINAL SIN. IT'S A SIMPLE CASE OF AN INDIVIDUAL AT ODDS WITH SOCIETY."

"HEY, GUYS — WAKE UP!"

"DON'T YOU SEE, WILBERT — THIS SYMBOLIC ACT CAN
SCAR YOU PSYCHOLOGICALLY FOR YEARS."

"YOU KNOW WHAT'LL DO WONDERS FOR YOU? A NOSE JOB."

"YOU MUST LEARN TO BE IN TOUCH WITH YOUR INNER TADPOLE."

I can't stop thinking about that movie I saw last night.
I can't stop thinking about that movie I saw last night.
I can't stop thinking about that movie I saw last night.
I can't stop thinking about that movie I saw last night.
I can't stop thinking...
S. Harris

COLLECTIVE MEMORY
I recall when I was a boy in Vienna— more than fifty years ago— a dog chased me into the lake...
OH, YES — I REMEMBER THAT!
S. Harris

"I HAVE TO CONVINCE HIM IT'S NOT GOING TO RUIN HIS MACHO IMAGE IF HE BUNTS."

EVERY ONCE IN A WHILE COLLECTIVE UNCONSCIOUS KICKS IN
I wish this was a cave and I had some fruit.
I'D JUST LIKE TO SIT IN A CAVE AND EAT FRUIT.
It would be cool to be in a cave and eat fresh fruit.
I'VE BEEN THINKING OF GOING TO A CAVE SOMEWHERE, AND EATING TROPICAL FRUIT.
I've been thinking of that myself.
S. Harris

"YOU CALL <u>THAT</u> ANXIETY?"

"See, my intensive-stress therapy really works. You are no longer concerned with your minor anxieties."

"THE REASON YOU'RE HYPERACTIVE IS THAT THERE'S JUST TOO MUCH OXYGEN IN THE ROOM."

"STOP TRYING TO PSYCHOANALYZE ME WHEN I'M TRYING TO PSYCHOANALYZE YOU."

"STOP SERVING THEM AS SOON AS THEY START TO BRING UP REPRESSED CHILDHOOD MEMORIES."

"THIS BABY WAS OWNED BY A VERY SELF-CONFIDENT PERSON WHO DID NOT THINK A LITTLE RUST AND A FEW DENTS WERE A THREAT TO HIS MANHOOD."

"I RECENTLY SAW THE MALTESE FALCON FOR THE FIRST TIME IN YEARS, AND I DIDN'T LIKE IT NEARLY AS MUCH AS I EXPECTED TO. BECAUSE OF THAT, I FIND I'LL NOW HAVE TO RE-THINK MY WHOLE LIFE."

"AFTER SPENDING ALL DAY IN THE THRONE ROOM, COMING BACK HERE IS ALWAYS SOMETHING OF A LETDOWN."

"I UTILIZE THE BEST FROM FREUD, THE BEST FROM JUNG AND THE BEST FROM MY UNCLE MARTY, A VERY SMART FELLOW."

"YOU MEAN YOUR BIG SMILE IS BOTTLED-UP AGGRESSION? MINE IS BOTTLED-UP HOSTILITY."

"RORSCHACH! WHAT'S TO BECOME OF YOU?"

"TO SUMMARIZE: THE VISUAL JOKE BRINGS ON A VERY FAST REACTION, BUT THE VERBAL JOKE IS MORE WIDELY QUOTED AND IS REMEMBERED LONGER."

"WE'VE RUN ALL THE TESTS, DOC, AND CAN'T FIND A THING WRONG WITH IT. IT MUST BE PSYCHOLOGICAL."